CW00535945

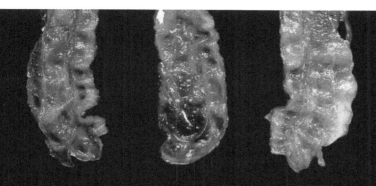

THE ULTIMATE
"Bacon"
COOKBOOK 2021

Over 100 quick and easy homemade recipes
for bacon you never knew you needed and
that are sure to become some favorite dishes
served at your table!

Richard
Duff

© Copyright 2021
All rights reserved.

The content contained within this book may not be reproduced, duplicated or transmitted without direct written permission from the author or the publisher.

Under no circumstances will any blame or legal responsibility be held against the publisher, or author, for any damages, reparation, or monetary loss due to the information contained within this book. Either directly or indirectly.

Legal Notice:

This book is copyright protected. This book is only for personal use. You cannot amend, distribute, sell, use, quote or paraphrase any part, or the content within this book, without the consent of the author or publisher.

Disclaimer Notice:

Please note the information contained within this document is for educational and entertainment purposes only. All effort has been executed to present accurate, up to date, and reliable, complete information. No warranties of any kind are declared or implied. Readers acknowledge that the author is not engaging in the rendering of legal, financial, medical or professional advice. The content within this book has been derived from various sources. Please consult a licensed professional before attempting any techniques outlined in this book.

By reading this document, the reader agrees that under no circumstances is the author responsible for any losses, direct or indirect, which are incurred as a result of the use of information contained within this document, including, but not limited to, errors, omissions, or inaccuracies.

TABLE OF CONTENTS

HOW IS BACON MADE?

Bacon has long been a favorite at breakfast tables and a great source of flavor for all sorts of dishes. With its rich, salty taste and crispy, melt-in-your-mouth texture, this versatile red meat is sure to hold onto its popularity for many years to come.

Even for the bacon-lovers among us, you may not know what exactly bacon is and how it's made. At S. Clyde Weaver, we're passionate about delicious cured meats and the traditional processes that go into preparing them, so we're going to take some time to explain what makes bacon that delicious meat we all know and love, and what all the labels mean that describe the various types of bacon you can buy today.

As we'll see, not all bacon delivers the superior quality and taste your ancestors were accustomed to, but some companies like S. Clyde Weaver are still committed to producing amazing bacon the traditional way.

WHAT IS BACON?

Bacon has been popular for centuries, especially in the West. Breeding pigs traditionally followed a seasonal schedule, with piglets being born in the spring, then being fattened up as they matured until they were ready to be slaughtered toward the end of the year. Since pork could be cured to create ham, bacon and more, it was an effective and tasty way of feeding families through the winter. In spite of modern refrigeration methods, people today still enjoy cured pork, including bacon.

With the exception of specialty products like turkey bacon that seek to imitate traditional pork bacon, real bacon is made from pork. Unlike some other types of pork you might purchase from the butcher or supermarket, bacon isn't defined by being from a specific cut of meat. Bacon can come from a pig's belly, back or sides — essentially anywhere that has an exceptionally high fat content. In the United Kingdom, back bacon is most common, but Americans are more familiar with "streaky" bacon, also known as side bacon, which is cut from pork belly.

Any of these cuts of meat could be sold fresh from the pig simply as pork belly, loin or sides to be cooked or as uncured bacon for people to cure with their own recipe and method. To turn the meat into bacon, it needs to go through a curing process, which we'll explain in detail in just a moment.

Jalapeno Poppers of Champions

Ingredients

18 fresh jalapeno peppers, halved lengthwise and seeded

1 (8 ounce) package cream cheese, softened

1 (5.25 ounce) package frozen vegetarian bacon strips, thawed toothpicks

Directions

- Preheat oven to 350 degrees F (175 degrees C). Spray a baking sheet with cooking spray.

- Fill each jalapeno half with cream cheese. Wrap 1 bacon strip around each jalapeno half and secure with a toothpick. Arrange wrapped jalapenos on baking sheet.

- Bake 12 minutes in preheated oven, or until bacon strips are crisp. Serve warm.

Corn with Bacon and Chili Powder

Ingredients

4 ears corn, husked and cleaned

4 slices bacon

4 dashes chili powder

Directions

- Wash the husked corn.

- Wrap one slice of bacon around each ear. It probably won't cover the entire ear, but be sure it goes from one end to the other.

- Sprinkle with chili powder to taste.

- Wrap the corn and bacon and chili powder in heavy aluminum foil and place over medium coals, or medium flame on gas grill.

- Cook approximately 20-25 minutes. Time will depend on the size of the ears of corn, and how fresh they are.

Carne en su Jugo (Meat in its Juices)

Ingredients

4 fresh tomatillos, husks removed

3 serrano chile peppers, seeded and chopped

1 clove garlic, peeled

3 cups water

6 slices bacon

2 pounds flank steak, cut into 1/2-inch squares

4 teaspoons chicken bouillon granules

2 (15.5 ounce) cans pinto beans 1/2 onion, chopped

6 tablespoons chopped fresh cilantro ground black pepper, to taste

1 lime, cut into 6 wedges

Directions

○ Combine the tomatillos, serrano peppers, garlic, and water in a small saucepan over medium-high heat; bring to a boil, cover, and simmer for 10 minutes. Remove the pan from the heat and allow to cool. Transfer the contents to a blender and blend until smooth. Set aside.

○ Cook the bacon in a large, deep skillet over medium-high heat until crispy, about 10 minutes. Drain on a paper towel-lined plate.

○ Crumble the bacon and set aside.

○ Place a non-stick skillet over medium-high heat; cook the flank steak in the hot skillet until completely browned. Pour the tomatillo mixture over the beef and bring to a boil. Stir the chicken bouillon into the mixture, and reduce heat to medium. Cover the skillet and simmer until tender, at least 30 minutes and up to 1 hour.

○ Meanwhile, heat the pinto beans in a saucepan over medium heat until warm; reduce heat to low to keep warm until needed. Stir the bacon and pinto beans into the flank steak mixture; divide the mixture between 6 bowls. Garnish each with onion, cilantro, black pepper, and a lime wedge.

Sunday Brunch Eggs

Ingredients

12 slices Canadian bacon

12 slices Swiss cheese

12 eggs

1 cup whipping cream

1/3 cup grated Parmesan cheese

12 slices toast (optional)

Directions

- Place Canadian bacon in a greased 13-in. x 9-in. x 2-in. baking dish; top with Swiss cheese. Carefully bread an egg over each piece of cheese.

- Pour cream over eggs and sprinkle with Parmesan cheese. Bake, uncovered, at 375 degrees F for 20-25 minutes or until eggs reach desired doneness.

- Let stand for 5 minutes. Cut between each egg; serve on toast if desired.

Red Rice and Sausage

Ingredients

2 cups long grain white rice

4 cups water

3 slices turkey bacon

1 onion, chopped

1 teaspoon minced garlic

1 green bell pepper, seeded and chopped

1 (16 ounce) package smoked turkey sausage, halved and sliced

1 (14.5 ounce) can stewed tomatoes, drained

1 (14 ounce) jar spaghetti sauce dried Italian seasoning to taste salt and pepper to taste

Directions

⤳ Combine the rice and water in a saucepan, and bring to a boil. Cover, reduce heat to low, and simmer for 15 to 20 minutes, until rice is tender and the water has been absorbed. Set aside.

⤳ Preheat the oven to 350 degrees F (175 degrees C).

⤳ Heat a large skillet over medium heat. Add the bacon, and brown on each side. Add the onion, garlic and green peppers to the skillet, and cook until soft, stirring frequently. Mix in the sausage, and cook until hot, then pour in the tomatoes. Cook just until heated through. Stir in the cooked rice and spaghetti sauce.

⤳ Season with Italian seasoning, salt and pepper. Transfer to a large casserole dish, and cover with a lid or aluminum foil.

⤳ Bake for 1 hour in the preheated oven, then remove the lid, and cook for an additional 15 minutes.

Penne with Pancetta, Tuna, and White Wine

Ingredients

3 tablespoons olive oil, divided

3 ounces pancetta bacon, diced

1 medium onion, chopped

1 clove garlic, minced

1/4 teaspoon crushed red pepper flakes

5 ounces fresh mushrooms, sliced 1/2 cup dry white wine

1/2 cup frozen green peas

12 cherry tomatoes, halved

5 ounces baby spinach

2 (6 ounce) cans solid white tuna packed in water, drained

1 tablespoon lemon juice salt and pepper to taste

1 pound penne pasta freshly grated Parmesan cheese

Directions

- Heat 1 tablespoon olive oil in a skillet over medium heat. Stir in pancetta, and cook until browned. Remove to paper towels.

- Return skillet to medium heat, and pour in 2 tablespoons olive oil.

- Stir in onion, garlic, and crushed red pepper. Cook until soft, about

- 5 minutes. Stir in mushrooms. Cook until they begin to give off juices.

- Turn the heat up to medium high, and pour in wine. Cook about 3 minutes.

- Reduce heat to medium low. Stir in peas, cherry tomatoes, and spinach. Flake in tuna, drizzle in lemon juice, and season with salt and pepper. Stir to combine, and cook until warmed through.

- Meanwhile, bring a large pot of salted water to boil. Cook penne until al dente, about 8 to 10 minutes. Drain, and stir into tuna mixture. Top with freshly grated Parmesan.

Jalapenos del Raton

Ingredients

1 (16 ounce) package spicy pork sausage

30 jalapeno peppers

1 (8 ounce) package cream cheese, softened

2 pounds turkey bacon toothpicks

Directions

- Preheat an outdoor grill for high heat. Lightly oil the grate.

- In a large skillet over medium heat, cook the sausage until browned. Drain excess grease, and set aside. Meanwhile, slice the peppers in half lengthwise, and remove and discard the seeds and membrane. Fill one half of each pepper with cream cheese, and the other half with sausage. Put the pepper halves back together, and wrap with a slice of bacon to hold. Secure bacon with a toothpick.

- Grill peppers for about 15 minutes, turning to ensure even cooking until bacon is crisp, and pepper is toasted. Let them cool down a bit, then eat 'em.

Velvety Pumpkin Soup With Blue Cheese and

Ingredients

2 (15 ounce) cans pumpkin

1 quart chicken stock

1 cup half-and-half

1 shallot, minced

1/4 cup molasses

2 tablespoons butter

1 teaspoon pumpkin pie spice

1 teaspoon salt

1/4 teaspoon cayenne pepper

6 slices bacon

1 cup crumbled blue cheese

Directions

- Stir together the pumpkin, chicken stock, half-and-half, shallot, molasses, butter, pumpkin pie spice, salt, and cayenne pepper in a large stockpot over low heat; simmer 10 minutes.

- Meanwhile, place bacon in a large skillet over medium-high heat, and cook until crispy; remove to paper towels to drain, then cool and crumble.

- Ladle soup into bowls. Top with bacon and blue cheese.

Iowa Corn Casserole

Ingredients

1 pound bacon, diced

2 cups bread crumbs

1/4 cup minced onion

1/2 cup chopped green pepper

2 (15 ounce) cans cream-style corn

Directions

⮥ In a skillet, fry the bacon until lightly browned. Remove and set aside. Pour 1/8 to 1/4 cup of bacon drippings over bread crumbs; set aside.

⮥ Discard all but 2 tablespoons of remaining drippings; saute onion and green pepper until tender. Stir in corn and bacon.

⮥ Spoon into a 1-qt. baking dish; sprinkle with crumbs. Bake at 350 degrees F for 20-25 minutes or until bubbly and heated through.

Herb, Garlic and Bacon Pork Loin

Ingredients

1 (5 pound) pork loin roast

1 tablespoon olive oil

1 pound sliced bacon

3 cups chicken stock

1 tablespoon dried rosemary

1 tablespoon dried thyme

6 fresh basil leaves

6 fresh sage leaves

4 cloves garlic, chopped

8 fresh pearl onions, peeled

Directions

- Preheat the oven to 300 degrees F (150 degrees C).

- Rub the pork loin with olive oil and place in a roasting pan. Drape slices of bacon over the top. Combine the chicken stock, rosemary, thyme, basil, sage and garlic. Pour over the roast.

- Place onions around the sides. Cover with a lid or aluminum foil.

- Bake for 1 hour and 30 minutes. Remove the lid or foil, and continue to bake for 30 minutes, or until the bacon is browned.

Sugar and Spice Bacon

Ingredients

1/2 cup all-purpose flour 1/2 cup brown sugar

1 teaspoon coarsely ground black pepper

1 pound thick cut bacon

Directions

- Preheat oven to 400 degrees F (200 degrees C).

- Place flour, sugar, and pepper into a resealable plastic bag and shake to mix. Shake bacon with flour mixture a few strips at a time to coat. Place coated bacon onto a baking sheet or broiler pan.

- Bake in preheated oven for 15 minutes or until bacon has cooked to desired doneness.

Yummy Quiche

Ingredients

8 ounces bacon

1 (9 inch) unbaked 9 inch pie crust

2 cups sharp Cheddar cheese, shredded

1 cup shredded Monterey Jack cheese

3 tablespoons all-purpose flour

5 eggs, lightly beaten

1 1/2 cups half-and-half 1/2 cup diced onion

1 (4 ounce) can diced green chile peppers, drained

Directions

⟳ Preheat oven to 350 degrees F (175 degrees C). Place bacon in a large, deep skillet. Cook over medium high heat until evenly brown. Drain, crumble and set aside.

⟳ Place crust in a 9 inch glass pie plate. Sprinkle bacon inside of crust. In a small bowl, combine Cheddar cheese, Monterey jack cheese and flour. In a separate bowl, beat together eggs, cream, onion and green chiles.

⟳ Add cheese mixture; stir well. Pour mixture into pie crust.

⟳ Bake in preheated oven for 60 to 70 minutes, until set. Let stand 10 minutes before serving.

Water Chestnuts a la Bacon

Ingredients

2 (8 ounce) cans water chestnuts   Wrap each water chestnut in 1 slice of bacon. When all chestnuts

1 pound bacon   are wrapped arrange them on a microwave-safe plate covered with paper towels.

Directions

- Cook the water chestnuts in a microwave on high for 5 to 8 minutes or until the bacon is cooked.

- Cool for a few minutes and serve.

Navy Bean Soup

Ingredients

1 (16 ounce) package dried navy beans water to cover

7 cups chicken stock 1/2 cup margarine

4 carrots, chopped

1 onion, chopped

1/2 pound bacon

Directions

- Clean and sort the beans. Place them in a large bowl with water to cover and soak for 3 hours.

- In a large pot over medium heat, combine the beans and the chicken stock and allow to simmer.

- Meanwhile, melt the butter or margarine in a large skillet over medium heat.

- Add the carrots and onion and saute for 10 minutes, or until onion is caramelized.

- Add this mixture to the pot.

- In the same skillet over medium high heat, saute the bacon for 10 to 15 minutes, or until it is crisp.

- Drain the grease and add the bacon to the pot.

- Continue to simmer the soup over medium heat, stirring frequently, until the beans are tender and the soup has thickened.

Curry Broccoli Salad

Ingredients

1/2 pound bacon

6 cups fresh broccoli florets 1/2 cup diced onion

1/2 cup dried cherries 1/2 cup sunflower seeds 3/4 cup mayonnaise

1 teaspoon curry powder

2 tablespoons cider vinegar 1/4 cup white sugar

Directions

- Place bacon in a large, deep skillet. Cook over medium high heat until evenly brown. Drain, crumble and set aside.

- In a large bowl, combine the bacon, broccoli, onion, dried fruit and sunflower seeds.

- Whisk together the mayonnaise, curry powder, vinegar and sugar.

- Pour dressing over salad; toss to coat, and marinate over night.

Hungry Man's Hash Browns

Ingredients

10 cups large chunks of peeled potatoes

8 slices bacon

3 large onions, sliced

1 1/2 teaspoons salt

Directions

- Place potatoes in large pot. Fill the pot with cold water until it is half an inch above the top of the potatoes. Add the salt to the water and stir briefly to dissolve. Bring water to a boil and cook until tender, about 15 to 20 minutes.

- Drain and set aside to cool.

- Place bacon in a large, deep skillet. Cook over medium high heat until evenly brown. Remove bacon, drain, cool and crumble. Leave bacon fat in skillet and return to stove.

- Add potato chunks, onion and crumbled bacon to skillet. Cook over medium high heat until potatoes begin to brown and onions are translucent, about 25 minutes.

Beef, Burgundy Style

Ingredients

1 cup beef broth

3 tablespoons all-purpose flour

1 tablespoon tomato paste

1 teaspoon beef demi glace

3 tablespoons bacon drippings

2 pounds beef round, cut into 3 inch pieces

3 tablespoons sherry wine

1 1/2 cups chopped onions

1 cup Burgundy wine

12 fresh mushrooms, sliced 1/4 cup butter

1 tablespoon chopped fresh parsley, for garnish

Herb Bouquet (Bouquet Garni)

3 sprigs fresh parsley

3 sprigs fresh rosemary

1 sprig fresh thyme

1 bay leaf

Directions

- In a small bowl, mix together beef broth, flour, tomato paste and demi glace; set aside.

- Heat bacon drippings in a large heavy skillet over medium heat. Add beef, and cook until brown on all sides.

- Remove beef from skillet; set aside. Stir the sherry wine into the skillet. Add the onions, and cook about 5 minutes.

- Blend in the tomato paste mixture, and bring to a rapid boil, stirring constantly. Stir in Burgundy wine.

- Make the herb bouquet: Place parsley, rosemary, thyme, and bay leaf in asquare of cheesecloth. Place herb bouquet in sauce.

- Return beef to skillet. Cover, and simmer over low heat for about 3 hours, or until beef is tender.

- Melt butter in a small skillet over medium heat. Saute mushrooms until lightly browned. Add to meat in the skillet, and continue cooking 15 minutes. Discard bouquet garni.

- Serve in a casserole dish, sprinkled with parsley.

Cajun Corn and Bacon Maque Choux

Ingredients

6 ears corn, husked and cleaned

2 tablespoons vegetable oil

1 large onion, thinly sliced

1 cup green bell pepper, chopped

1 large fresh tomato, chopped 1/4 cup milk

salt to taste

cayenne pepper

1/4 cup chopped green onions

8 strips crisply cooked bacon, crumbled

Directions

- Cut corn off the cobs by thinly slicing across the tops of the kernels; place in a medium bowl. Cut across the kernels again to release milk from the corn, add milk to bowl. Set aside.

- Heat the oil in a large skillet over medium-high heat. Add onion and green pepper, cook until onion is transparent, about 5 to 8 minutes. Combine corn, tomatoes, and milk with the onion mixture. Reduce heat to medium low, and cook 20 minutes longer, stirring frequently to prevent sticking. Do not boil.

- Season with salt and cayenne pepper. Lower heat, cover skillet, and cook 5 to 10 minutes longer. Stir in green onions and bacon. Remove from heat and serve.

Hot Spinach and Artichoke Dip

Ingredients

8 slices bacon

1 (10 ounce) package frozen chopped spinach, thawed and drained

1 (14 ounce) can quartered marinated artichoke hearts, drained

1 (5 ounce) container garlic-herb flavored cheese spread

1 cup grated Parmesan cheese

1 (8 ounce) container sour cream 1/2 cup mayonnaise

Directions

- Preheat oven to 400 degrees F (200 degrees C).

- Place bacon in a large, deep skillet. Cook over medium high heat until evenly brown. Drain and crumble into a medium bowl.

- Mix spinach, artichoke hearts, garlic-herb flavored cheese spread, Parmesan cheese, sour cream and mayonnaise into the bowl with bacon.

- Scoop mixture into a 7x11 inch baking dish. Bake in the preheated oven 20 minutes, or until bubbly and lightly browned.

Chicken Thigh and Dumpling Stew

Ingredients

3 tablespoons butter

2 pounds chicken thighs

8 slices bacon

2 stalks celery, chopped

3 carrots, chopped

1 red onion, finely chopped

3 cloves garlic, finely chopped

1 (14 ounce) can vegetable broth 1/2 teaspoon paprika

1/2 cup heavy cream

1 (26 ounce) can condensed cream of chicken soup

1 cup water

1 (8.75 ounce) can sweet corn, drained ground black pepper to taste

1 (10 ounce) can buttermilk biscuits

Directions

- In a large skillet over medium-high heat, melt the butter and cook the chicken thighs until the meat is just cooked through.

- Remove the chicken pieces from the skillet and allow to cool. Using forks, pull meat from the bones and cut into small pieces or shred. Set aside.

- Meanwhile, in a medium skillet, cook the bacon over medium heat until nicely browned and crispy.

- Remove strips from bacon grease and drain on a paper towel. Crumble the drained and cooled bacon and set aside.

- Reserve 1 tablespoon of the bacon drippings.

- Scrape the chicken drippings from the large skillet into a large stock pot or Dutch oven. Cook the celery, carrots, red onion, and garlic over medium heat until the red onions are soft and transparent.

- Add the vegetable broth, chicken, and 1 tablespoon reserved bacon grease.

- Simmer over medium heat for 12 minutes, then stir in paprika, heavy cream, cream of chicken soup, and water.

- Heat through, stirring regularly, about 5 minutes. Stir in the sweet corn and ground pepper.

- Tear each buttermilk biscuit into quarters and drop into the chicken stew.

- Reduce heat to medium-low; stir occasionally until dough is cooked though, forming dumplings at the top of the stew, about 10 minutes.

- Remove from heat and serve with a garnish of crumbled bacon.

Crab-Stuffed Filet Mignon with Whiskey

Ingredients

CRAB STUFFING:

2 tablespoons olive oil

1 teaspoon minced onion

1 teaspoon minced green onion

1 teaspoon minced garlic

1 teaspoon minced celery

1 teaspoon minced green bell pepper

2 tablespoons shrimp stock or water

1 (6 ounce) can crab meat, drained

2 tablespoons bread crumbs

1 teaspoon Cajun seasoning

PEPPERCORN SAUCE

1 1/4 cups beef broth

1 teaspoon cracked black pepper

1 fluid ounce whiskey

1 cup heavy cream

STEAKS:

4 (6 ounce) filet mignon steaks

4 slices bacon, cooked lightly salt and cracked black pepper to taste

1 tablespoon olive oil

1 clove garlic, minced

1 teaspoon minced shallot

1 cup crimini mushrooms, sliced

1 fluid ounce whiskey

1 teaspoon Dijon mustard

Directions

- Make Crab Stuffing: Heat 2 tablespoons olive oil in a large skillet. Saute onion, green onion, garlic, celery, and green pepper until tender.

- Stir in shrimp stock, crab meat, bread crumbs, and Cajun seasoning. Remove from heat, and set aside.

- Prepare Peppercorn Sauce: In a small saucepan over medium heat, combine beef broth and cracked black pepper.

- Simmer until reduced to 1 cup, stirring frequently. Add 1 ounce whiskey and 1 cup cream. Continue simmering until reduced to 1 cup.

- Remove from heat, and set aside.

- Prepare Steaks: Slice a pocket into the side of each steak, and stuff generously with crab stuffing.

- Wrap bacon around side, and secure with toothpicks.

- Season to taste with salt and pepper; set aside. Heat olive oil in a large cast iron skillet over medium heat.

- Saute garlic and shallot for 1 minute. Stir in mushrooms, and saute until tender. Remove mushroom mixture, and set aside.

- Place steaks in skillet, and cook to desired doneness. Remove from skillet, and keep warm.

- Deglaze skillet with 1 ounce whiskey.

- Reduce heat, and stir in peppercorn sauce and Dijon mustard.

- Add mushroom mixture, and reduce sauce until thickened.

- Remove toothpicks and bacon from steaks, and arrange steaks on a plate. Top with sauce.

Green Beans with Almonds

Ingredients

2 pounds fresh green beans, washed and trimmed

2 slices bacon

1/4 cup sliced almonds

Directions

- Remove both ends of beans, break in half, and wash thoroughly.

- Place in a large pot and add water 3 to 4 inches from the top.

- Add bacon and cook until tender.

- Remove bacon from cooking water and discard.

- Remove beans and place in a large bowl, add almonds and toss. Serve Hot.

Spicy Collard Greens

Ingredients

6 slices bacon

1 bunch collard greens, rinsed and trimmed

1/3 cup vinegar salt to taste ground black pepper to taste ground cayenne pepper to taste

Directions

- Place bacon in a large, deep skillet. Cook over medium high heat until evenly brown.

- Bring a large pot of water to a boil. Add collard greens, bacon (with grease), vinegar, salt, black pepper and cayenne pepper.

- Boil until greens are tender, about 30 minutes.

Hunter Style Chicken

Ingredients

4 tablespoons olive oil

1 (3 pound) whole chicken, cut into pieces

6 slices bacon, diced

2 onions, chopped

1 cup fresh sliced mushrooms

1 tablespoon chopped fresh parsley

1 tablespoon chopped fresh basil

1 teaspoon salt

freshly ground black pepper

1 cup white wine

1 pound tomatoes, diced

Directions

- Heat oil in a large skillet; brown chicken; remove. Add bacon and saute over medium heat for about 2 minutes.

- Add onions and mushrooms and continue to saute until onions are translucent. Return chicken to skillet; sprinkle with parsley, basil, salt and pepper.

- Add wine and tomatoes. Cover and let simmer for

- 25 to 30 minutes, turning chicken once during cooking. Remove chicken from skillet and pour sauce over chicken.

Green Bean Bundles II

Ingredients

2 (15 ounce) cans whole green beans, drained

1 cup Italian-style salad dressing

9 slices bacon, cut in half

Directions

- In a medium bowl combine green beans and dressing; toss gently. Cover and chill overnight.

- Preheat oven to Broil. Place a rack high in the oven, about 5 inches from the top.

- Drain beans; arrange in bundles of 10 to 12 beans each.

- Wrap half a slice of bacon around each bundle, and secure with a toothpick.

- Place bundles on a baking sheet and broil for 7 minutes, or until bacon is cooked.

Chicken Salad with Bacon, Lettuce and Tomato

Ingredients

3 cups chopped cooked chicken breast

5 slices bacon

2 stalks celery, chopped

1 cup chopped fresh tomato 3/4 cup mayonnaise

1 tablespoon chopped fresh parsley

2 tablespoons chopped green onion

1 teaspoon lemon juice

1 dash Worcestershire sauce salt and pepper to taste

12 leaves romaine lettuce

1 avocado - peeled, seeded and sliced

Directions

- Place bacon in a large, deep skillet. Cook over medium high heat until evenly brown. Drain, crumble and set aside to cool.

- Prepare the dressing by mixing together the mayonnaise, parsley, green onions, lemon juice, Worcestershire sauce, salt and pepper.

- In a medium bowl, stir together the chicken breast, tomatoes and bacon. Pour dressing over chicken mixture and toss well to coat. Refrigerate until chilled; serve over lettuce leaves and garnish with avocado slices.

Garlic, Basil, and Bacon Deviled Eggs

Ingredients

12 eggs

5 slices bacon

2 large cloves garlic, pressed 1/2 cup finely chopped fresh basil 1/3 cup mayonnaise

1/4 teaspoon crushed red pepper flakes salt and pepper to taste

1/4 teaspoon paprika for garnish

Directions

- Place the eggs into a saucepan in a single layer and fill with water to cover the eggs by 1 inch. Cover the saucepan and bring the water to a boil over high heat.

- Remove from the heat and let the eggs stand in the hot water for 15 minutes. Drain. Cool the eggs under cold running water. Peel once cold. Halve the eggs lengthwise and scoop the yolks into a bowl.

- Mash the yolks with a fork.

- Cook the bacon in a large, deep skillet over medium-high heat until evenly browned, about 10 minutes. Drain on a paper towel-lined plate; chop once cool.

- Add to the mashed egg yolks. Stir the basil, mayonnaise, red pepper flakes, salt, and pepper into the mixture until evenly mixed.

- Fill the egg white halves with the mixture; sprinkle each stuffed egg with a bit of paprika.

Party Chicken I

Ingredients

4 skinless, boneless chicken breasts

4 slices bacon

1 (4 ounce) jar dried beef

1 cup sour cream

1 (10.75 ounce) can condensed cream of chicken soup

Directions

- Shred beef, and spread into the bottom of a greased 8-inch square baking dish.

- Wrap each chicken breast with 1 strip of bacon, and lay on top of beef.

- Mix together undiluted soup and sour cream. Pour over chicken.

- Bake at 350 degrees F (175 degrees C) for 45 minutes to 1 hour.

New Orleans Jambalaya

Ingredients

1 cup soy sauce

4 tablespoons dried thyme

1 teaspoon cayenne pepper

2 tablespoons paprika

2 onions, chopped

2 tablespoons ground black pepper

16 skinless, boneless chicken breast halves

3/4 pound bacon, cut into small pieces

8 onions, diced

4 cloves garlic, minced

6 tablespoons all-purpose flour

3 pounds chorizo, sliced into chunks

3 pounds cooked ham, cut into 1/2 inch pieces

3 tablespoons dried thyme

4 teaspoons cayenne pepper

5 cups chicken stock

6 (14.5 ounce) cans peeled and diced tomatoes with juice

4 green bell pepper, chopped

6 cups uncooked white rice

10 pounds medium shrimp -peeled and deveined

Directions

Chicken Marinade

- In a large, shallow glass baking dish, mix together soy sauce, 4 tablespoons dried thyme, 1 teaspoon cayenne pepper, 2 tablespoons paprika, 2 chopped onions and 2 tablespoons black pepper.

- Place the chicken in the marinade.

- Refrigerate for at least 3 hours.

Saute bacon in a Dutch oven over medium heat until brown.

- Add the onion and garlic.

- Continue to cook 5 minutes.

- Mix in flour and sausage.

- Cook 5 minutes more; stirring frequently.

- Add the ham, thyme, cayenne, chicken stock, tomatoes, reserved juice and green peppers and bring to boil. Stir in rice and cover.

- Cook for 25minutes.

- Remove from heat and cool completely and refrigerate.

- Two hours before you intend to serve the jambalaya, discard marinade and bake chicken breasts at 500 degrees F (250 degrees C) for 12 minutes, or until the flesh is firm when pressed with finger. Remove from oven.

- Cool and slice into bite-size pieces.

- Reduce oven's temperature to 250 degrees F (120 degrees C). Place covered jambalaya on large baking tray filled with to water. Bake until warm, about 2 hours.

- Just before serving the jambalaya, boil 5 quarts of water.

- Add the shrimp and cook for 3 minutes until they are firm to the touch.

- Drain well. Toss shrimp and chicken with jambalaya mixture and serve.

Jalapeno Pepper Appetizers

Ingredients

10 jalapeno peppers

4 ounces cream cheese, softened

10 bacon strips, halved

Directions

- Cut peppers in half lengthwise; remove seeds, stems and center membrane.

- Stuff each half with about 2 teaspoons of cream cheese.

- Wrap with bacon and secure with toothpick.

- Place on a broiler rack that has been coated with non-stick cooking spray.

- Bake at 350 degrees F for 20-25 minutes or until bacon is crisp.

- Remove toothpicks. Serve immediately.

Nana White's Famous Brussels Sprouts

Ingredients

2 1/2 pounds Brussels sprouts

12 slices bacon, diced

1/2 cup chopped onion

3 tablespoons all-purpose flour

1 1/2 cups milk

1/3 cup dry white wine 1/2 teaspoon salt

1/2 teaspoon dried oregano

3/4 teaspoon dried dill weed

1/8 teaspoon black pepper

Directions

- Preheat oven to 325 degrees F (165 degrees C).

- Cut an X in the stem end of the Brussels sprouts. Bring a pot of water to a boil.

- Add Brussels sprouts and cook until tender, about 7 to 10 minutes.

- Drain and place in a shallow baking dish.

- Meanwhile, place bacon in a large, deep skillet. Cook over medium high heat until evenly brown.

- Drain, reserving 1 tablespoon of grease, and set aside.

- Saute onion in reserved bacon grease, until limp.

- Stir in flour and cook until bubbly. Remove from heat and whisk in milk.

- Return to heat and cook, stirring, until the mixture boils and thickens.

- Stir in wine, salt, oregano, dill, pepper, and all but 2 tablespoons of bacon.

- Pour mixture evenly over the Brussels sprouts and sprinkle with remaining bacon.

- Bake in preheated oven for 20 minutes, or until heated through.

Quiche Lorraine I

Ingredients

1 recipe pastry for a 9 inch single crust pie

6 slices bacon

1 onion, chopped

3 eggs, beaten

1 1/2 cups milk

1/4 teaspoon salt

1 1/2 cups shredded Swiss cheese

1 tablespoon all-purpose flour

Directions

- Preheat oven to 450 degrees F (230 degrees C).

- Line pastry with a double layer of aluminum foil. Bake in preheated oven for 8 minutes. Remove foil and bake for 4 to 5 minutes more, or until crust is set. Reduce oven temperature to 325 degrees F (165 degrees C).

- Place bacon in a large, deep skillet. Cook over medium high heat until evenly brown. Remove bacon from pan, crumble and set aside. Reserve 2 tablespoons bacon grease in skillet.

- Cook onion in reserved drippings until tender; drain and set aside.

- In a large bowl, mix together eggs, milk and salt. Stir in bacon and onion. In a separate bowl, toss cheese and flour together.

- Add cheese to egg mixture; stir well. Pour mixture into hot pastry shell.

- Bake in preheated oven for 35 to 40 minutes, or until knife inserted into center comes out clean. If necessary, cover edges of crust with foil to prevent burning.

- Let quiche cool for 10 minutes before serving.

Kidney Bean Coleslaw

Ingredients

4 cups shredded cabbage 1/2 cup real bacon bits

1 (16 ounce) can kidney beans, rinsed and drained

2 celery ribs, thinly sliced

2/3 cup chopped onion

4 teaspoons minced fresh parsley 1/2 cup mayonnaise

2 tablespoons cider vinegar 1/4 teaspoon pepper

1/8 teaspoon salt

Directions

- In a large bowl, combine the cabbage, bacon, beans, celery, onion and parsley.

- In a small bowl, combine the mayonnaise, vinegar, pepper and salt; pour over cabbage mixture and toss to coat.

- Cover and refrigerate for 2-3 hours. Stir before serving.

Jen's Nine Layer Dip

Ingredients

2 skinless, boneless chicken breast halves

1 1/2 tablespoons chopped fresh cilantro

1 tablespoon vegetable oil

4 slices lean bacon, chopped

1 (16 ounce) can refried beans

1 teaspoon taco seasoning mix

1 cup sour cream

3/4 cup shredded Cheddar cheese

1 cup prepared guacamole

1 cup diced tomatoes

1 1/2 tablespoons chopped fresh cilantro

2 tablespoons sliced black olives

2 tablespoons finely sliced green onions

1/4 cup shredded Cheddar cheese

Directions

- Place the chicken, 1 1/2 tablespoons of cilantro, and vegetable oil in a skillet over medium heat, and pan-fry the chicken breasts until lightly golden brown, no longer pink in the middle, and the juices run clear, about 5 minutes per side.

- Remove the chicken and set aside. When cooled, cut into cubes.

- Place the bacon in the same skillet, and cook over medium-high heat, stirring often, until evenly browned, about 10 minutes. Mix the refried beans into the skillet with the bacon, and cook, stirring frequently, until the beans are hot and bubbling, 5 to 10 minutes. Mix the taco seasoning and sour cream together in a bowl.

- To assemble, spread the hot bean and bacon mixture into the bottom of an 8x8-inch glass dish. Sprinkle the chicken cubes over the bean mixture, then follow with these layers: 3/4 cup of Cheddar cheese, guacamole, sour cream mixture, and sliced tomatoes.

- Sprinkle the top with 1 1/2 tablespoons of cilantro, black olives, green onions, and 1/4 cup of shredded cheddar cheese.

Collard Greens and Beans

Ingredients

3 slices bacon, coarsely chopped

1 red onion, thinly sliced

2 tablespoons minced garlic, or to taste

5 cups collard greens, stems and center ribs discarded and leaves chopped

3/4 cup water, or as needed

1 tablespoon brown sugar

2 teaspoons cider vinegar

1 teaspoon crushed red pepper flakes, or to taste

salt and black pepper to taste

1 (15 ounce) can cannellini beans, drained and rinsed

Directions

- Place the bacon in a large, deep pan with a lid, and cook over medium-high heat, stirring occasionally, until evenly browned, about 10 minutes. Remove the bacon pieces from the pan, and set aside.

- Reduce the heat to medium-low, and stir the sliced onion into the hot bacon fat. Cook and stir the onion until it begins to brown, scraping the bits off the bottom of the pan, about 8 minutes.

- Add the garlic, and cook and stir 4 more minutes. Return the bacon to the pan, stir in the collard greens, and toss gently until the greens are wilted, about 3 minutes.

- Pour in the water to almost cover the collard greens, and stir in the brown sugar, vinegar, crushed red pepper, and salt and pepper. Bring to a boil, cover, reduce heat to low, and simmer the collard greens until very tender, 1 to 2 hours.

- About 1/2 hour before serving, stir in the cannellini beans into the collard greens, and return to a simmer.

Bacon, Asparagus, and Cheese Sandwiches

Ingredients

8 slices bacon

1 (10 ounce) can asparagus tips, drained

4 thick slices sourdough bread, lightly toasted

4 slices sharp Cheddar cheese

Directions

- Adjust oven rack to upper position, and set oven to broil. You may also use a toaster oven to cook the sandwiches if you don't want to broil them in the oven.

- Place bacon in a large, deep skillet. Cook over medium high heat until evenly brown and crispy. Drain on paper towels.

- Place a few spears of asparagus on a slice of bread. Top with 2 slices crisp bacon then a slice of cheese.

- Toast under the broiler until the cheese is melted and bubbly.

Breakfast Burritos

Ingredients

12 slices bacon, diced

12 eggs, lightly beaten

salt and pepper to taste

10 (8 inch) flour tortillas

1 1/2 cups shredded Cheddar cheese

1/2 cup thinly sliced green onions

Directions

- In a skillet, cook bacon until crisp; remove to paper towels. Drain, reserving 1-2 tablespoons drippings. Add eggs, salt and pepper to drippings; cook and stir over medium heat until the eggs are completely set.

- Spoon about 1/4 cup of egg mixture down the center of each tortilla; sprinkle with cheese, onions and bacon.

- Fold bottom and sides of tortilla over filling. Wrap each in waxed paper and aluminum foil.

- Freeze for up to 1 month.

- To use frozen burritos: Remove foil. Place waxed paper-wrapped burritos on a microwave-safe plate.

Microwave at 60% power for 1

- 1/2 to 2 minutes or until heated through. Let stand for 20 seconds.

Fried Cabbage with Bacon, Onion, and Garlic

Ingredients

6 slices bacon, chopped

1 large onion, diced

2 cloves garlic, minced

1 large head cabbage, cored and sliced

1 tablespoon salt, or to taste

1 teaspoon ground black pepper 1/2 teaspoon onion powder

1/2 teaspoon garlic powder 1/8 teaspoon paprika

Directions

- Place the bacon in a large stockpot and cook over medium-high heat until crispy, about 10 minutes.

- Add the onion and garlic; cook and stir until the onion caramelizes; about 10 minutes.

- Immediately stir in the cabbage and continue to cook and stir another 10minutes.

- Season with salt, pepper, onion powder, garlic powder, and paprika.

- Reduce heat to low, cover, and simmer, stirring occasionally, about 30 minutes more.

3B-C (Best Baked Bean Casserole)

Ingredients

1 tablespoon butter

1 small onion, diced 1/2 pound bacon

1 (28 ounce) can baked beans (such as Bush's OriginalB®)

2 teaspoons Worcestershire sauce

1 tablespoon ketchup

1 teaspoon prepared yellow mustard

1 cup brown sugar, divided

Directions

- ⊃ Preheat an oven to 400 degrees F (200 degrees C).

- ⊃ Melt the butter in a skillet over low heat.

- ⊃ Cook and stir until the onion has softened and turned translucent, 10 to 15 minutes.

- ⊃ Meanwhile, place the bacon in a large, deep skillet, and cook over medium-high heat, turning occasionally, until evenly browned, about 10 minutes.

- ⊃ Drain the bacon slices on a paper towel-lined plate.

- ⊃ Cut bacon into bite-sized pieces and set aside.

- ⊃ Combine the baked beans, Worcestershire sauce, ketchup, mustard, and onions in a 2-quart casserole dish. Stir in 2/3 of the cooked bacon and 1/4 of the brown sugar until evenly mixed.

- ⊃ Cover the bean mixture with the remaining bacon, and sprinkle with the remaining brown sugar.

- ⊃ Bake in the preheated oven until hot and bubbly, about 45 minutes.

Crescent Bacon Cheese Tartlet

Ingredients

1 (8 ounce) can PillsburyB® refrigerated crescent dinner rolls or PillsburyB® Crescent Recipe Creationsв and refrigerated flaky dough sheet

1/3 cup shredded Swiss cheese

1/4 cup chopped cooked bacon

1 tablespoon chopped green onion

1 egg

3 tablespoons whipping cream

Directions

- ➲ Heat oven to 375 degrees F.

- ➲ If using crescent rolls: Unroll dough into 1 large rectangle on work surface. Press into 12x9-inch rectangle, firmly pressing perforations to seal. If using dough sheet: Unroll dough on work surface. Press into 12x9-inch rectangle.

- ➲ Cut dough into 12 squares. Gently press squares into 12 ungreased mini muffin cups, shaping edges to form rims 1/4 inch high. Spoon cheese evenly into dough-lined cups.

- ➲ Top each with bacon and onion. In small bowl, beat egg and whipping cream with wire whisk or fork until blended.

- ➲ Spoon slightly less than 1 tablespoon mixture into each cup.

- ➲ Bake 15 to 20 minutes or until edges are golden brown and filling is set. Cool 5 minutes. Remove from muffin cups.

Hot German Potato Salad I

Ingredients

6 potatoes

4 large eggs

1 pound bacon

1 medium head escarole

1/4 cup apple cider vinegar

Directions

- Bring a large pot of salted water to a boil.

- Add potatoes and cook until tender but still firm, about 15 minutes. Drain, cool and chop.

- Place eggs in a saucepan and cover with cold water.

- Bring water to a boil; cover, remove from heat, and let eggs stand in hot water for 10 to 12 minutes. Remove from hot water, cool, peel and chop.

- Place bacon in a large, deep skillet. Cook over medium high heat until evenly brown. Drain, crumble and set aside.

- Reserve bacon drippings.

- Place potatoes in skillet with reserved bacon dripping, fry until heated through.

- Add escarole, bacon, eggs and vinegar.

- Cook until escarole becomes wilted and serve warm.

Corn Chowder - Fast and Great

Ingredients

5 slices bacon, diced

1 large onion, chopped

4 medium potatoes, peeled and cubed

5 cups chicken broth

1/2 teaspoon dried oregano salt and pepper to taste

1 (11 ounce) can cream-style corn

1 (10 ounce) can whole kernel corn, drained

1/2 cup heavy cream

1/2 cup shredded Monterey Jack cheese

1/2 cup shredded Cheddar cheese

Directions

- In a large pot over medium-high heat, cook and stir the bacon until crisp.

- Drain off grease, leaving about 1 tablespoon in the pot.

- Break the bacon into pieces in the pot.

- Place the onion in the pot, and cook until transparent. Mix in the potatoes, and cook until lightly browned on the outside. Stir in the chicken broth, and season with oregano, salt and pepper.

- Cover and simmer over low heat for about 30 minutes, or until the potatoes are soft.

- Pour in the cream-style corn and whole kernel corn, and cook for 10 more minutes.

- Stir in the cream, Monterey Jack cheese, and Cheddar cheese over low heat. Do not boil.

- Remove from the heat, and serve.

Deer Poppers

Ingredients

1 pound venison steaks, cubed

1/2 teaspoon Greek seasoning, or to taste

1/4 teaspoon steak seasoning, or to taste

1 (16 ounce) bottle Italian salad dressing

1/2 cup jalapeno pepper slices

10 slices bacon, cut in half toothpicks, soaked in water

Directions

- Season the venison meat with Greek seasoning and steak seasoning. Place in a bowl, and pour in enough Italian dressing to cover.

- Refrigerate for at least 2 hours to marinate, but preferably overnight. Preheat the grill for medium heat. Drain the marinade from the meat, and discard the marinade. Place a slice of jalapeno on top of a piece of meat, then wrap with a slice of bacon. Secure with a soaked toothpick. Repeat with remaining meat.

- Grill the deer poppers for 15 to 20 minutes, turning occasionally to brown the bacon. Serve and enjoy!

Anniversary Chicken II

Ingredients

1 pound thick cut bacon

1 onion, chopped

1 tablespoon olive oil

6 skinless, boneless chicken breast halves

1/2 cup stir-fry sauce

1 cup Ranch-style salad dressing

1 cup grated Parmesan cheese

Directions

- Preheat oven to 350 degrees F (175 degrees C).

- Heat a large skillet to medium heat and fry bacon until crisp.

- Drain and pat dry with paper towels; set aside.

- In the same skillet, saute onion in bacon fat until tender.

- Add to bacon and set aside.

- In a separate large skillet, heat oil over medium high heat and brown chicken breasts.

- Place browned chicken in a lightly greased 9x13 inch baking dish; pour stir-fry sauce over chicken, then spoon salad dressing onto each breast.

- Sprinkle with cheese, and top with the bacon mixture.

- Bake in preheated oven for 30 minutes or until chicken is cooked through and juices run clear.

Ultimate Green Beans

Ingredients

2 slices bacon, diced

1/2 white onion, minced

1 pound fresh green beans, trimmed

1/2 teaspoon red pepper flakes 1/2 cup boiling water

1 tablespoon butter

1 teaspoon lemon juice salt and pepper to taste

Directions

- Cook the bacon in a large, deep skillet over medium-high heat until crisp, about 10 minutes.

- Remove the bacon with a slotted spoon and drain on a paper towel-lined plate; return the skillet with the reserved bacon grease to the stove.

- Cook the onion in the bacon drippings until soft, 5 to 7 minutes. Stir in the green beans and red pepper flakes; cook another 2 minutes.

- Pour the boiling water into the skillet and cover the skillet immediately; steam for about 15 minutes, shaking the skillet occasionally to keep the beans from sticking to the bottom.

- Add the butter, lemon juice, salt, and pepper; cook and stir until the butter is melted, 3 to 5 minutes.

- Sprinkle the cooked bacon over the beans to serve.

Chorizo Filled Dates

Ingredients

1 chorizo sausage link

12 pitted dates

3 slices bacon, cut into fourths

2 cups vegetable oil for frying (optional)

1 egg, beaten (optional)

1 teaspoon water (optional)

1/4 cup all-purpose flour (optional)

Directions

- Cut the ends off of the chorizo, and cut into 12 cubes.

- Stuff each piece inside one of the dates.

- Wrap a piece of bacon around each date, and secure with toothpicks.

- This part may all be done ahead of time.

- Heat a skillet over medium-high heat. Place the dates in the pan with the bacon seam side down. Fry until golden, then turn and fry on the other side until bacon is cooked through.

- You may serve them now, or proceed to coat and fry them.

- Heat the oil in a deep-fryer or large skillet to 375 degrees F 190 degrees C.

- Whisk together the egg and water in a small bowl. Coat the dates with flour, then dip into the egg.

- Place immediately into the hot oil, and fry until golden, turning once.

- This will take about 4 minutes total. Drain and serve right away.

Spinach Ranch Salad

Ingredients

4 cups baby spinach, rinsed and dried

1/2 cup cucumber

1 cup broccoli florets

1/2 cup feta cheese, crumbled 1/4 red onion, chopped

2 small, cooked chicken breast, cut into small pieces bacon bits

1/2 cup ranch dressing

Directions

- Toss together spinach, cucumber, broccoli, feta, onion, chicken, and bacon in a large bowl.
- Pour dressing over salad, and gently toss again.

Western Range Sandwiches

Ingredients

4 bacon strips, diced

1 pound lean ground beef

1 medium onion, chopped

1/2 cup chopped green pepper

2 (16 ounce) cans kidney beans, rinsed and drained

1 (8 ounce) can tomato sauce

2 tablespoons chili powder 1/2 teaspoon salt

1/8 teaspoon pepper

2 cups shredded Cheddar cheese

6 English muffins, split and toasted

Directions

- In a large skillet, cook bacon until crisp.

- Remove to paper towels.

- Drain, reserving 2 tablespoons of drippings.

- Cook beef, onion and green pepper in drippings until meat is no longer pink.

- Add beans, tomato sauce, chili powder, salt, pepper and bacon.

- Bring to a boil. Reduce heat; add cheese.

- Cook and stir over low heat until cheese is melted.

- Spoon into English muffins halves.

Texas Brunch

Ingredients

6 eggs

8 ounces bacon 1/4 cup butter

1/4 cup all-purpose flour

2 cups milk

2 cups shredded Cheddar cheese 1/2 cup sour cream

1 teaspoon cayenne pepper

1 teaspoon salt

1/2 teaspoon black pepper

6 cornbread

1 cup shredded Cheddar cheese

6 green onions, chopped

Directions

- Place eggs in a saucepan and cover with cold water. Bring water to a boil and immediately remove from heat. Cover and let eggs stand in hot water for 10 to 12 minutes. Remove from hot water, cool, peel and chop.

- Place bacon in a large, deep skillet. Cook over medium high heat until evenly brown. Drain, crumble and set aside.

- In a medium sized saucepan, melt butter over medium heat. When butter has melted, whisk in the flour. Stir until all lumps have dissolved.

- Slowly pour in the milk, stirring constantly, until thickened.

- As gravy begins to thicken, add chopped eggs and 2 cup cheese. Cook 3 to 5 minutes to melt the cheese and heat through. Stir in the sour cream, cayenne, salt and pepper; stir until heated through.

- Keep warm over low heat until ready to serve (do not boil). Slice cornbread pieces and lay open on serving plates.

- Ladle a generous amount of egg mixture over the cornbread, top with remaining shredded cheese, crumbled bacon, and green onion.

Cornmeal Waffle Sandwiches

Ingredients

3/4 cup all-purpose flour 3/4 cup cornmeal

1 tablespoon baking powder

1 tablespoon sugar

1 teaspoon salt

2 eggs, separated

1 cup milk

3 tablespoons butter or margarine, melted

1/2 cup shredded Cheddar cheese

Mayonnaise

12 bacon strips, cooked and drained

2 small tomatoes, sliced

salt and pepper to taste

Directions

- In a mixing bowl, combine the first five ingredients. In another bowl, beat egg yolks.

- Add milk and butter; stir into dry ingredients just until moistened.

- Stir in cheese. In a small mixing bowl, beat egg whites until stiff peaks form; fold into the batter.

- Bake 12 waffles in a preheated waffle iron according to manufacturer's directions until golden brown.

- Spread mayonnaise on six waffles; top each with bacon, tomato, salt, pepper and remaining waffles.

- Serve immediately.

Figs with Goat Cheese, Pecans and Bacon

Ingredients

6 figs, halved

6 ounces goat cheese

1/2 cup toasted, chopped pecans

3 slices bacon, cut in half

Directions

- Preheat the broiler.

- Stuff fig halves with goat cheese. Press pecans into the cheese. Wrap each stuffed fig half with half a slice of bacon, securing with toothpicks.

- Arrange on a medium baking sheet.

- Broil 5 minutes, or until bacon is evenly brown and crisp and goat cheese is bubbly and lightly browned.

Smokey Black Beans

Ingredients

1 pound dry black beans, soaked overnight

4 teaspoons bacon drippings

1 onion, chopped

2 teaspoons hickory-flavored liquid smoke

2 tablespoons dark molasses

1/2 cup packed brown sugar

4 slices pickled jalapeno peppers

Directions

- Drain the black beans from their soaking water and place in a slow cooker. Fill with enough fresh water to cover them. Cover and set to High.

- Heat bacon drippings in a skillet over medium heat. Add onions; cook and stir until tender. Stir this into the beans along with the brown sugar, liquid smoke, molasses and jalapeno slices.

- Stir to blend, then cover and cook on High for 5 to 6 hours, or until beans are tender.

Triple Bypass

Ingredients

1 pound ground beef

2 (15 ounce) cans chili with beans

1 (32 ounce) package extra crispy frozen potato rounds (such as Tater Tots®)

4 slices bacon (optional)

1 (8 ounce) package processed cheese food (such as Velveeta®)

4 green onions, chopped (optional)

Directions

◌ Preheat an oven to 450 degrees F (230 degrees C).

◌ Heat a large skillet over medium-high heat and stir in the ground beef.

◌ Cook and stir until the beef is crumbly, evenly browned, and no longer pink. Drain and discard any excess grease.

◌ Stir in the chili and mix thoroughly. Spread the chili mixture into a 9x13-inch baking pan then top with a single layer of the frozen potato rounds.

◌ Bake in the preheated oven until heated through and potato rounds are crisp, 18 to 22 minutes. Meanwhile, place the bacon in a large, deep skillet, and cook over medium-high heat, turning occasionally, until evenly browned, about 10 minutes. Drain the bacon slices on a paper towel-lined plate. Crumble bacon and set aside.

◌ Melt the processed cheese food in a microwave-safe glass or ceramic bowl in 30-second intervals, stirring after each melting, for 1 to 3 minutes (depending on your microwave).

◌ Pour melted cheese food over the potato rounds and top with bacon and chopped green onions.

Swiss Cheese Scramble

Ingredients

1 pound bacon

1 cup bread cubes

2 3/4 cups milk

12 eggs

salt and pepper to taste 1/4 cup butter

1 pound Swiss cheese, shredded

4 teaspoons butter, melted

1 cup dry bread crumbs

Directions

- Place bacon in a large, deep skillet. Cook over medium-high heat until evenly brown.

- Drain, crumble and set aside.

- In a large bowl, Combine the bread cubes and milk. Drain after 5 minutes.

- In a separate bowl, beat together milk, eggs, salt and pepper.

- In a large skillet or saucepan, melt 1/4 cup butter over medium heat. Add the egg mixture and scramble until soft. Do not fully cook.

- Add the soaked bread cubes and turn into a greased 9x13 inch baking pan. Sprinkle shredded cheese on top of casserole.

- In a small bowl, stir together butter and bread crumbs.

- Sprinkle this mixture over the cheese and then top with the bacon. Cover and refrigerate overnight.

- The next morning, preheat oven to 350 degrees F (175 degrees C).

- Bake in preheated oven for 40 minutes.

- Serve warm.

Quick Quiche

Ingredients

8 slices bacon

4 ounces shredded Swiss cheese

2 tablespoons butter, melted

4 eggs, beaten

1/4 cup finely chopped onion

1 teaspoon salt

1/2 cup all-purpose flour

1 1/2 cups milk

Directions

- Place bacon in a large, deep skillet. Cook over medium high heat until evenly brown. Drain, crumble and set aside.

- Preheat oven to 350 degrees F (175 degrees C).

- Lightly grease a 9 inch pie pan.

- Line bottom of pie plate with cheese and crumbled bacon. Combine eggs, butter, onion, salt, flour and milk; whisk together until smooth; pour into pie pan.

- Bake in preheated oven for 35 minutes, until set. Serve hot or cold.

Wild Rice Soup IV

Ingredients

2 pounds bacon

1 cup uncooked wild rice

2 cups water

1/2 cup chopped onion

1/2 cup chopped celery

1/2 cup chopped green bell pepper

1 (10.75 ounce) can condensed cream of mushroom soup

1 (10.75 ounce) can condensed cream of chicken soup

2 (14.5 ounce) cans chicken broth

3 1/2 cups water

Directions

- In a small sauce pan, cook rice with two cups of water until tender; set aside.

- Fry the bacon until crisp.

- Drain, but reserve 5 tablespoons of the grease. Crumble bacon and set aside.

- Fry the onions, celery and green peppers in the bacon grease until the onions are translucent.

- Transfer the vegetables, rice and crumbled bacon to a 5 quart pan. Stir in the mushroom and chicken soups, chicken broth and remaining 3 1/2 cups of water.

- Simmer over medium heat for one hour to blend all of the flavors.

Bacon Onion Turnovers

Ingredients

3 (.25 ounce) packages active dry yeast

1/2 cup warm water (110 degrees F to 115 degrees F)

1 cup warm milk (110 to 115 degrees F)

1/2 cup butter or margarine, melted

2 teaspoons salt

3 1/2 cups all-purpose flour

1/2 pound sliced bacon, cooked and crumbled

1 large onion, diced

1 egg, lightly beaten

Directions

- In a large mixing bowl, dissolve yeast in warm water.

- Add the milk, butter and salt; beat until smooth. Stir in enough flour to form a soft dough.

- Turn onto a floured surface; knead until smooth and elastic, about 6-8 minutes.

- Place in a greased bowl, turning once to grease top. Cover and let rise in a warm place until doubled, about 30 minutes.

- Punch dough down. Turn onto a lightly floured surface; divided into 30 pieces.

- Roll each into a 4-in. circle.

- Combine bacon and onion; place about 2 teaspoons on one side of each circle. Fold dough over filling; press edges with a fork to seal.

- Place 3 in. apart on greased baking sheets.

- Cover and let rise in a warm place until doubled, about 20 minutes.

- Brush with egg. Bake at 425 degrees F for 10-15 minutes or until golden brown. Remove to wire racks.

- Serve warm.

Shredded Brussels Sprouts

Ingredients

1/2 pound sliced bacon 1/4 cup butter

2/3 cup pine nuts

2 pounds Brussels sprouts, cored and shredded

3 green onions, minced 1/2 teaspoon seasoning salt pepper to taste

Directions

- Place bacon in a large, deep skillet.

- Cook over medium-high heat until crisp. Drain, reserving 2 tablespoons grease, crumble and set aside.

- In the same skillet, melt butter in with reserved bacon grease over medium heat. Add pine nuts, and cook, stirring until browned.

- Add Brussels sprouts and green onions to the pan, and season with seasoning salt and pepper.

- Cook over medium heat until sprouts are wilted and tender, 10 to 15 minutes. Stir in crumbled bacon just before serving.

Okra and Tomatoes

Ingredients

2 slices bacon

1 pound frozen okra, thawed and sliced

1 small onion, chopped

1/2 green bell pepper, chopped

2 celery, chopped

1 (14.5 ounce) can stewed tomatoes

salt and pepper to taste

Directions

- Place bacon in a large, deep skillet. Cook over medium high heat until evenly brown.

- Drain, crumble and set aside.

- Remove bacon from pan and saute okra, onion, pepper and celery until tender.

- Add tomatoes, salt and pepper and cook until well blended.

- Garnish with crumbled bacon, if desired.

Grilled Deli Sandwiches

Ingredients

1 medium onion, sliced

1 cup sliced fresh mushrooms

1 cup julienned green pepper

1 cup julienned sweet red pepper

2 tablespoons vegetable oil

12 slices sourdough bread

1/2 pound thinly sliced deli honey ham, smoked turkey and pastrami

6 bacon strips, cooked and crumbled

6 slices process American cheese

6 slices Swiss cheese

Directions

- In a large skillet, saute the onion, mushrooms and peppers in oil until tender.

- Layer six slices of bread with ham, turkey, pastrami, bacon, vegetables and cheese; top with remaining bread.

- Wrap each sandwich in foil.

- Grill, uncovered, over medium heat for 4-5 minutes on each side or until heated through.

Onion Tart

Ingredients

1/4 cup butter

1 1/2 pounds onions, sliced

2 eggs, beaten

1 (9 inch) pie crust, baked

4 slices bacon

Directions

- Preheat oven to 350 degrees F (175 degrees C).
- In a large skillet, melt butter and saute onions until soft. Remove from heat.
- Place bacon in a large, deep skillet.
- Cook over medium high heat until evenly brown.
- Drain, crumble and set aside.
- Mix in eggs.
- Pour into prepared shell and bake at 350 degrees F (175 degrees C) for approximately 20 minutes.
- Top with bacon, can be served warm or cold.

Pasta Carbonara I

Ingredients

1/2 pound bacon, cut into small pieces

4 eggs, room temperature 1/4 cup heavy cream at room temperature

1 cup grated Parmesan cheese

16 ounces dry fettuccine pasta 1/4 cup butter, softened

1/4 cup chopped parsley

ground black pepper to taste

Directions

- Cook bacon until crisp. Drain on paper towels.
- In medium bowl beat together eggs and cream just until blended. Stir in cheese and set aside.
- Cook pasta according to package directions. Drain and return to pan. Toss with butter until it is melted.
- Add bacon and cheese mixture and toss gently until mixed.

Broccoli Salad II

Ingredients

1/2 pound bacon

2 heads fresh broccoli, chopped

1 bunch green onions, chopped 1/2 cup shredded carrots

salt and pepper to taste

1 cup mayonnaise

1/2 cup distilled white vinegar 1/2 cup raisins (optional)

Directions

- Place bacon in a large, deep skillet. Cook over medium high heat until evenly brown. Drain, crumble and set aside.

- In a large bowl, combine the bacon, broccoli, green onions, carrots and salt and pepper.

- In a small bowl whisk together the mayonnaise and vinegar. Pour dressing over vegetables and toss to coat evenly.

- Chill for 1 hour before serving.

Filet Mignon with Bacon Cream Sauce

Ingredients

4 (4 ounce) beef tenderloin filets

1 teaspoon olive oil

3 slices bacon, chopped

1 tablespoon butter

4 shallots, diced

1/4 cup half-and-half cream salt and pepper to taste

Directions

- Preheat an outdoor grill for medium-high heat, and lightly oil the grate.

- Brush the filets with olive oil, and cook on the preheated grill to desired doneness (about 4 minutes per side for medium rare).

- An instant-read thermometer inserted into the center should read 130 degrees F (54 degrees C). Set the steaks aside on a platter tented with aluminum foil to rest.

- While the steaks are resting, prepare the sauce: cook and stir the chopped bacon in a small saucepan over medium heat until the bacon pieces are crisp, 3 to 5 minutes.

- Stir in the butter and shallots, and cook and stir until the shallots are soft and translucent, about 5 minutes more.

- Stir in the half-and-half, bring the mixture to a simmer over medium-low heat, and cook, stirring occasionally, until the sauce is slightly thickened, about 8 minutes.

- Season to taste with salt and pepper, and serve over the steaks.

Feta Cheese and Bacon Stuffed Breasts

Ingredients

8 tablespoons olive oil

2 teaspoons lemon juice

4 cloves crushed garlic

1 tablespoon dried oregano salt and pepper to taste

4 skinless, boneless chicken breasts

4 slices feta cheese

4 slices bacon, fried and drained

Directions

- Preheat oven to 350 degrees F (175 degrees C).

- In a small bowl combine the oil, lemon juice, garlic, oregano, salt and pepper.

- Mix together.

- Place chicken in a 9x13 inch baking dish and pour oil mixture over chicken.

- Stuff each chicken breast with 1 slice feta cheese and 1 slice bacon.

- Secure open sides with toothpicks.

- Bake uncovered at 350 degrees F (175 degrees C) for 30 to 35 minutes.

Southern Coleslaw

Ingredients

1 tablespoon red wine vinegar

1 teaspoon white sugar 1/3 cup mayonnaise

1 tablespoon coarse-grain brown mustard

1 head cabbage, cored and shredded

2 hard-cooked eggs, peeled and chopped

6 slices crisply cooked bacon, crumbled

salt and pepper to taste

Directions

- In a large bowl, stir together the vinegar, sugar, mayonnaise and mustard.
- Add the cabbage, eggs and bacon, and toss lightly to coat with the dressing.
- Season with salt and pepper.
- Refrigerate for 1 hour before serving to blend flavors.

Bacon Wrapped Smokies

Ingredients

1 pound sliced bacon, cut into thirds

1 (14 ounce) package beef cocktail wieners

3/4 cup brown sugar, or to taste

Directions

- Preheat the oven to 325 degrees F (165 degrees C).

- Refrigerate 2/3 of the bacon until needed. It is easier to wrap the wieners with cold bacon.

- Wrap each cocktail wiener with a piece of bacon and secure with a toothpick.

- Place on a large baking sheet. Sprinkle brown sugar generously over all.

- Bake for 40 minutes in the preheated oven, until the sugar is bubbly.

- To serve, place the wieners in a slow cooker and keep on the low setting.

Irish Potato Soup

Ingredients

1 (1 pound) package bacon

1 onion, chopped

1 cup celery, chopped

6 potatoes, scrubbed and cubed salt and pepper to taste

2 (12 fluid ounce) cans evaporated milk

Directions

- Place the bacon in a large, deep skillet, and cook over medium-high heat, turning occasionally, until evenly browned, about 10 minutes.

- Drain the bacon slices on a paper towel-lined plate, crumble, and set aside.

- Cook and stir onion and celery in the remaining bacon grease over medium heat until the onion is translucent and tender.

- Drain excess grease, then stir in potatoes.

- Add water to cover all but 1 inch of the potatoes.

- Bring to a boil over medium-high heat, then reduce to medium-low, and simmer until potatoes are tender, about 15 minutes, stirring often.

- Stir in the evaporated milk, and continue cooking until warmed through.

- Season with salt and pepper.

- Stir in bacon just before serving.

Potato Pizza

Ingredients

2 cups instant mashed potato flakes

1 (8 ounce) package shredded Cheddar cheese, divided

1 (3 ounce) jar real bacon bits

1 bunch green onions, chopped

1 (10 ounce) can pizza crust dough

1/2 cup sour cream

Directions

- Preheat the oven to 425 degrees F (200 degrees C).

- Prepare instant mashed potatoes according to package directions.

- Stir in half of the Cheddar cheese, bacon bits, and green onions.

- Cut the pizza crust dough in half, and spread into the bottom of two 8-inch round pans.

- Bake for 4 minutes in the preheated oven, until about halfway done. Spoon the potato mixture over each crust.

- Sprinkle remaining Cheddar cheese over the top.

- Bake for an additional 5 minutes in the preheated oven, until crust is golden, and cheese is melted.

- Let cool for 5 minutes before slicing and serving.

- Top with sour cream to taste.

Easy Seven Layer Vegetable Salad

Ingredients

1 head lettuce, torn into small pieces

1 (10 ounce) package frozen green peas, thawed

1/2 cup chopped green bell pepper

12 slices bacon

1 1/2 cups small cauliflower florets 1/2 cup chopped celery

2 cups mayonnaise

3 tablespoons white sugar

4 ounces shredded Cheddar cheese

Directions

- Place bacon in a large, deep skillet. Cook over medium high heat until evenly brown. Drain and set aside. In a 9x13 inch pan layer the lettuce followed by the peas, green pepper, bacon, cauliflower and celery.

- In a small bowl combine the mayonnaise and the sugar. Spread mixture over salad. Sprinkle cheese over top. Cover and chill for at least 8 to 12 hours before serving.

Bacon and Cheese Tartlets

Ingredients

1 (9.5 ounce) package Pepperidge Farm® Mini Puff Pastry Shells

1 cup shredded Cheddar cheese 1/3 cup mayonnaise

2 medium green onions, chopped

3 slices bacon, cooked and crumbled

1/8 teaspoon cracked black pepper

Directions

- Bake, cool and remove the "top" of the shells according to the package directions. Reduce the oven temperature to 350 degrees F.

- Stir the cheese, mayonnaise, green onions and bacon in a small bowl.

- Divide the cheese mixture among the shells.

- Bake for 5 minutes or until hot.

Hot German Potato Salad II

Ingredients

3 pounds potatoes

1 pound bacon, cubed

1 onion, diced

2 cups white sugar

2 cups white wine vinegar

Directions

- Bring a large pot of salted water to a boil.

- Add potatoes and cook until tender but still firm, about 15 minutes.

- Drain, cool and chop.

- Place bacon and onion in a large, deep skillet. Cook over medium heat until bacon is evenly brown.

- Drain excess grease from skillet.

- Add the sugar and vinegar to the bacon and onion mixture and bring to a boil. Pour the mixture over the potatoes and stir.

Glorified Hot Dogs

Ingredients

1 large whole dill pickle

4 ounces Cheddar or Colby cheese

8 hot dogs

4 teaspoons prepared mustard

8 bacon strips

8 hot dog buns

Directions

- Cut pickle lengthwise into eight thin slices.

- Cut cheese into eight 5-in. x 1/2-in. x 1/4-in. sticks.

- Cut hot dogs in half lengthwise; spread cut surfaces with mustard.

- On eight hot dog halves, layer a pickle slice and a cheese stick; top with remaining hot dog halves.

- Place one end of a bacon stop at the end of each hot dog; push a toothpick through the bacon and both hot dog pieces.

- Firmly wrap bacon around each hot dog and secure at the other end with a toothpick.

- Grill, uncovered, over medium heat for 8-10 minutes or until bacon is completely cooked, turning occasionally.

- Discard toothpicks.

- Serve in buns.

Down Home Chicken

Ingredients

1 (4 pound) whole chicken, cut into 6 pieces

4 cups buttermilk

1 teaspoon salt

1 teaspoon freshly ground black pepper

1/4 teaspoon cayenne pepper 1/4 teaspoon dried thyme

2 cups all-purpose flour

1 teaspoon white sugar

5 cups shortening for frying 1/4 cup bacon grease

Directions

- Place the cut up chicken into a large resealable bag or a 9x13 inch casserole dish.

- Pour the buttermilk over the chicken, seal or cover and refrigerate for 24 hours.

- Remove the chicken from the buttermilk. In a bowl, stir together the salt, black pepper, cayenne pepper, thyme, flour and sugar; pour onto a plate.

- Heat the shortening and bacon drippings in a large skillet or electric skillet to 365 degrees F (185 degrees C). Dredge the chicken in the flour mixture and place it into the hot fat.

- Fry on one side for 10 minutes, then turn and fry 10 minutes on the reverse side. If softer skin is desired, cover the skillet for the last 10 minutes.

- Remove and drain on brown paper grocery bags. (The smaller pieces will be finished first. The chicken is done when the juices run clear.)

Bacon-Mustard Salad Dressing

Ingredients

1 bacon, diced

6 tablespoons orange juice

1/2 cup fat-free sour cream

3 tablespoons finely chopped

green onions (white portion only)

1 tablespoon Dijon mustard

1 garlic clove, minced

2 teaspoons brown sugar 1/4 teaspoon salt

1/8 teaspoon pepper

Directions

- In a nonstick skillet, cook bacon over medium heat until crisp.

- Remove with a slotted spoon to drain on paper towels. Add orange juice to the drippings; stir to loosen browned bits from pan.

- Place the remaining ingredients in a blender or food processor; add orange juice mixture and bacon.

- Cover and process until smooth.

- Store in the refrigerator.

Linguine with Spinach and Brie

Ingredients

1 (8 ounce) package uncooked linguine pasta

4 slices bacon, cut in half

2 cups baby spinach, rinsed and dried

1 clove garlic, minced 1/4 cup cubed Brie cheese extra virgin olive oil

Directions

- Bring a large pot of lightly salted water to boil. Add linguine, and cook until al dente, about 8 to 10 minutes.

- Drain, and set pasta aside.

- Fry bacon in a large skillet over medium heat until crisp.

- With a slotted spoon, remove bacon to paper towels.

- Stir garlic into bacon fat, and cook until garlic is slightly browned, about 1 to 2 minutes.

- Add spinach, and toss until spinach begins to wilt, about 2 minutes.

- Remove skillet from heat, stir in pasta, and toss.

- Sprinkle with Brie and drizzle with olive oil to taste, then toss until cheese is melted.

Bacon Wrapped Water Chestnuts IV

Ingredients

1 pound bacon

2 (8 ounce) cans water chestnuts, drained

1 cup mayonnaise

1/2 cup white sugar

3 tablespoons dill pickle relish 1/2 cup ketchup

Directions

- ⮑ Preheat oven to 425 degrees F (220 degrees C).

- ⮑ Wrap single pieces of bacon around individual water chestnuts, securing with a toothpick.

- ⮑ Place the wrapped water chestnuts on a large baking sheet. Bake in the preheated oven 20 minutes, or until the bacon is crisp. Remove from heat and drain.

- ⮑ In a medium bowl, mix the mayonnaise, white sugar, dill pickle relish and ketchup. Pour the mixture over the wrapped water chestnuts.

- ⮑ Bake in the preheated oven 10 minutes, or until the sauce is hot and bubbly.

Quick Onion Kuchen

Ingredients

2 tablespoons butter

4 large onions, sliced

4 slices rye bread

2 eggs

1 cup sour cream

1/4 teaspoon salt

ground white pepper, to taste

1/2 teaspoon caraway seeds

4 slices bacon

THE ULTIMATE BACON COOKBOOK 2021

Directions

- Preheat oven to 350 degrees F (175 degrees C.)

- Heat butter in a large skillet.

- Saute the sliced onions until soft and translucent; set aside.

- Line a 10 inch quiche pan with bread. Place cooked onions in an even layer over the bread.

- In a small bowl, combine eggs, sour cream, salt, white pepper and caraway seeds.

- Pour egg mixture over bread and onions, then lay bacon strips over top.

- Bake in the preheated oven 25 to 30 for minutes, or until filling is set.

Farmhouse Omelets

Ingredients

4 bacon strips, diced

1/4 cup chopped onion

6 eggs

1 tablespoon water 1/4 teaspoon salt

1/8 teaspoon pepper

1 dash hot pepper sauce

3 teaspoons butter, divided

1/2 cup cubed fully cooked ham, divided

1/4 cup thinly sliced fresh mushrooms, divided

1/4 cup chopped green pepper, divided

1 cup shredded Cheddar cheese, divided

Directions

- In a skillet, cook bacon over medium heat until crisp.

- Remove with a slotted spoon to paper towels.

- Drain, reserving 2 teaspoons drippings.

- In drippings, saute onion until tender; set aside.

- In a bowl, beat the eggs, water, salt if desired, pepper and pepper sauce.

- Melt 1-1/2 teaspoons butter in a 10-in. nonstick skillet over medium heat; add half of the egg mixture.

- As the eggs set, lift edges, letting uncooked portion flow underneath.

- When eggs are set, sprinkle half of the bacon, onion, ham, mushrooms, green pepper and cheese on one side; fold over.

- Cover and let stand for 1-2 minutes or until cheese is melted.

- Repeat with remaining ingredients for second omelet.

Pate Recipe

Ingredients

1 pound bacon strips, diced

3 medium onions, chopped

3 cloves garlic

1 pound chicken livers, trimmed and chopped

1 pound veal, trimmed and cubed

1 cup heavy cream

1/2 cup milk

3/4 cup butter

1 pinch salt and pepper to taste

Directions

- Place bacon in a large skillet over medium-high heat.

- Cook until wilted, then add the onion and whole garlic cloves.

- Cook, stirring constantly until the onion is soft.

- Add the chicken livers and veal cubes to the skillet, and cook until no longer pink. Set aside to cool.

- Line a 9x5 inch loaf pan or mold with waxed paper, or spray with cooking spray, and set aside.

- Spoon the meat mixture into the container of a food processor, and pulse until finely chopped.

- Do not puree. Melt the butter in a large skillet over medium heat. Add the meat mixture, and stir in heavy cream and milk.

- Cook until heated through. Season with salt and pepper to taste, then pour into the loaf pan or mold.

- Chill for at least 4 hours before serving.

South Jersey Oyster Pie

Ingredients

1/2 pound bacon

1 double crust ready-to-use pie crust

1 small onion, chopped

3 stalks celery, chopped

3 cloves garlic, minced

1 small green bell pepper, chopped

3 tablespoons all-purpose flour 3/4 cup heavy cream

24 oysters, shucked with liquid reserved

1/2 teaspoon seafood seasoning (such as Old Bay®), or more to taste

Directions

- Cook the bacon in a large, deep skillet over medium-high heat until golden brown, about 10 minutes; remove to a paper towel-lined plate to drain, reserving the drippings. Crumble the bacon.

- Preheat an oven to 350 degrees F (175 degrees C).

- Line a 9-inch pie pan with 1 of the pie crusts.

- Heat 1 tablespoon of the reserved bacon drippings in a skillet over medium-low heat; add the onion, celery, garlic, and green pepper to the hot drippings, cover, and cook until tender, about 5 minutes. Remove the cooked vegetables to a bowl.

- Increase heat to medium and stir 3 tablespoons of the reserved drippings and the flour together in the skillet to make a thick paste.

- Slowly pour the cream and 1 cup of the reserved liquid from the oysters into the paste; cook and stir until a thick gravy form.

- Fold the bacon, oysters, and vegetables into the mixture; season with seafood seasoning.

- Pour the mixture into the prepared pie crust. Cover with the remaining crust.

- Bake in the preheated oven until golden brown, about 30 minutes.

Southern-Style Crowder Peas

Ingredients

4 slices bacon

1 small onion, chopped

1 small green bell pepper, chopped

1 (16 ounce) package frozen crowder peas

2 cups water

1 tablespoon garlic powder

1 pinch dried thyme

1 crushed bay leaf

1/2 teaspoon seasoned salt to taste

2 slices cooked ham, cubed

1 tablespoon chopped fresh parsley

Directions

- Place bacon in a skillet over medium-high heat, and cook until evenly brown.

- Drain and crumble. Mix onion and green bell pepper into the skillet, and cook until tender.

- Stir in peas and water. Season with garlic powder, thyme, bay leaf, and seasoned salt.

- Bring to a boil. Reduce heat to low, and simmer 30 to 40 minutes, until peas are tender.

- Mix ham into the skillet. Adjust seasonings to taste.

- Continue cooking 5 minutes.

- Stir in fresh parsley just before serving.

Savory Venison Meatloaf

Ingredients

1 pound ground venison 1 egg

1 (4 ounce) packet saltine

crackers, finely crushed

1/4 cup barbecue sauce

1/2 yellow onion, chopped

1/2 teaspoon dried sage

1/2 teaspoon steak seasoning

2 tablespoons brown sugar

2 tablespoons Worcestershire sauce

3 slices bacon

3/4 cup barbecue sauce

2 tablespoons brown sugar

1 tablespoon Worcestershire sauce

Directions

- Preheat an oven to 350 degrees F (175 degrees C).

- Mix the venison, egg, cracker crumbs, 1/4 cup barbecue sauce, onion, sage, steak seasoning, 2 tablespoons brown sugar, and 2 tablespoons Worcestershire sauce in a mixing bowl with your hands until evenly combined.

- Pack into a 3x7-inch loaf pan, and lay the bacon strips over top.

- Bake in the preheated oven until no longer pink in the center and the bacon is crispy, about 35 minutes.

- An instant-read thermometer inserted into the center should read at least 160 degrees F (70 degrees C).

- Meanwhile, stir 3/4 cup barbecue sauce, 2 tablespoons brown sugar, and 1 tablespoon Worcestershire sauce in a sauce pan over medium heat. Simmer 5 minutes, whisking constantly.

- Pour the sauce over the cooked meatloaf, and let rest 5 minutes before serving.

Beer and Maple Lentil Stew

Ingredients

6 slices bacon, diced

1 cup diced onion

1 clove garlic, minced

1 cup diced celery

1 cup diced carrot

3 cups beef stock

1 (12 ounce) bottle beer

1 cup dried brown lentils, rinsed and drained

1 tablespoon maple syrup 1/4 teaspoon ground nutmeg 1/4 teaspoon caraway seed 1/4 teaspoon celery salt

salt and ground black pepper to taste

Directions

- Place a large pot over medium-high heat; cook the bacon in the pot until crisp, 5 to 7 minutes.

- Stir in the onion and garlic; continue to cook until onions are translucent, about 5 minutes.

- Stir in the celery and carrot; cook another 2 minutes.

- Pour the beef stock and beer into the pot; bring to a boil.

- Stir in the lentils, syrup, nutmeg, caraway seed, and celery salt; cover and cook for 45 minutes.

- Season with salt and pepper.

Cream Soup Base

Ingredients

1/2 cup butter

6 tablespoons all-purpose flour

2 cups milk

2 cubes chicken bouillon

ground black pepper to taste

Directions

- Melt butter in a saucepan.

- Add flour and make a paste.

- Add milk and bouillon cubes.

- Cook over low heat until thickened.

- Add pepper to taste.

- Add more milk when adding the other soup ingredients, depending on the thickness you desire.

- To this base you may add steamed broccoli and American cheese; or chunks of baked potato (peel and all) with American cheese, bacon pieces, and chives; or pureed, stewed tomatoes for a bisque; or leeks that have been cleaned well, steamed, and chopped; or cooked asparagus cut in pieces (if canned asparagus is used, add some of the liquid as well), topped with grated cheese and bacon pieces.

Bacon-Wrapped Peanut Butter Jalapenos

Ingredients

8 jalapeno peppers, halved lengthwise and seeded

1/2 cup peanut butter

8 slices bacon, cut in half

Directions

- Preheat oven to 350 degrees F (175 degrees C).

- Fill each jalapeno half with peanut butter and with a piece of bacon; secure the bacon with a toothpick.

- Arrange the wrapped jalapenos on a baking sheet.

- Bake in the preheated oven until the bacon is dark brown, about 25 minutes.

Rolled Flank Steak

Ingredients

1 (2 pound) beef flank steak 1/4 cup soy sauce

1/2 cup olive oil

2 teaspoons steak seasoning

8 ounces thinly sliced provolone cheese

4 slices thick cut bacon

1/2 cup fresh spinach leaves

1/2 cup sliced crimini mushrooms 1/2 red bell pepper, seeded and cut into strips

Directions

- Place the flank steak on a cutting board with the short end closest to you.

- Starting from one of the long sides, cut through the meat horizontally to within 1/2 inch of the opposite edge. (You can also ask your butcher to butterfly the flank steak for you instead of cutting it yourself.)

- Mix the soy sauce, olive oil, and steak seasoning together in a gallon-sized resealable plastic bag.

- Marinate flank steak in the refrigerator 4 hours to overnight.

- Preheat oven to 350 degrees F (175 degrees C).

- Grease a glass baking dish.

- Lay out the flank steak flat in front of you with the grain of the meat running from left to right.

- Layer the provolone across the steak, leaving a 1-inch border.

- Arrange the bacon, spinach, red pepper, and mushrooms across the cheese covered steak in stripes running in the same direction as the grain of the meat.

- Roll the flank steak up and away from you, so that

when the roll is cut into the pinwheel shape, each of the filling ingredients can be seen.

- Roll firmly, but be careful not to squeeze the fillings out the ends.

- Once rolled, tie every 2 inches with kitchen twine.

- Place in prepared baking dish, and bake in preheated oven for one hour, or until the internal temperature reaches 145 degrees F (65 degrees C).

- Remove from the oven and let rest for 5 to 10 minutes before cutting into 1 inch slices.

- Be sure to remove the twine before serving!

Slow Cooker Fifteen Bean Soup

Ingredients

1 large, meaty ham hock

4 slices bacon, diced

3 onions, chopped

3 carrots, diced

1 small head cabbage, shredded

3 tablespoons chili powder

1 clove garlic, minced

1 (8 ounce) package 15 bean mixture, soaked overnight

1 (28 ounce) can crushed tomatoes

1 teaspoon chopped fresh sage salt and pepper to taste

Directions

⮞ Place the ham hock in a 5 to 6 quart slow cooker, and fill half way full with water. Set to High.

⮞ Heat a large skillet over medium heat. Cook the bacon for a few minutes, then add onions, carrots, and cabbage.

⮞ Cook, stirring frequently for about 5 minutes. Stir in chili powder and garlic; cook for 2 more minutes.

⮞ Transfer the mixture to the slow cooker, and add beans, tomatoes, and sage.

⮞ Cover, and cook 2 hours on High. Reduce heat to Low, and cook for 6 to 7 hours, or until beans are tender.

⮞ Transfer ham hock to a cutting board, remove meat from bone, and return meat to slow cooker.

⮞ Season with salt and fresh ground pepper to taste.

Father-in-Law's Scallops with Sun-Dried

Ingredients

4 slices double smoked bacon

1 1/2 tablespoons olive oil

12 large scallops, patted dry 1/2 cup dry white wine

3 tablespoons sun-dried tomatoes packed in oil, drained and thinly sliced

1/4 cup heavy cream

2 tablespoons butter, at room temperature

2 teaspoons minced garlic

1 (8 ounce) package angel hair pasta

salt and black pepper to taste

Directions

- Place the bacon in a large, deep skillet, and cook over medium-high heat, turning occasionally, until evenly browned, about 10 minutes.

- Drain the bacon slices on a paper towel-lined plate.

- Chop the bacon, and set aside.

- Bring a large pot of lightly salted water to a boil for the pasta.

- While water is coming to a boil, heat olive oil in a large, heavy skillet over high heat, and pan-fry the scallops until browned and opaque, about 2 minutes per side. Remove scallops to a plate.

- Stir the angel hair pasta into the boiling water, and return to a boil.

- Cook the pasta uncovered, stirring occasionally, until the pasta has cooked through, but is still firm to the bite, 4 to 5 minutes.

- Drain well in a colander set in the sink, and divide the hot pasta between 4 plates.

- Pour white wine and sun-dried tomatoes into the skillet, and scrape up and dissolve any browned flavor bits left in the pan.

- Stir in the cream, bring to a boil over medium heat, reduce heat, and simmer until thickened, about 2 minutes.

- Remove the pan from the heat, and add the butter and garlic.

- Whisk the butter into the sauce, return the scallops to the pan, and cover with sauce.

- Spoon scallops and sauce over the pasta, sprinkle with chopped bacon, and season to taste with salt and pepper.

Bacon Broccoli Salad

Ingredients

10 bacon strips, cooked and crumbled

1 cup fresh broccoli florets 1/2 cup raisins

1/2 cup sunflower seeds 1/2 cup mayonnaise

1/4 cup sugar

2 tablespoons vinegar

Directions

- In a medium bowl, combine bacon, broccoli, raisins and sunflower seeds; set aside.

- Mix together mayonnaise, sugar and vinegar; pour over broccoli mixture and toss to coat.

- Cover and chill for 1 hour.

- Stir before serving.

Spaghetti Carbonara I

Ingredients

1 pound spaghetti

1 pound bacon, chopped

4 eggs, well beaten

1 cup grated Parmesan cheese 1/4 cup olive oil

Directions

- Bring a large pot of lightly salted water to a boil. Add pasta and cook for 8 to 10 minutes or until al dente; drain.

- Meanwhile, place bacon in a large, deep skillet. Cook over medium high heat until evenly brown. Drain, reserving some of the drippings, crumble and set aside.

- Scramble eggs in bacon drippings.

- Place spaghetti in a large bowl. Pour in olive oil, and mix well; use enough to just moisten spaghetti. Stir in bacon, eggs, and Parmesan cheese.

- Serve immediately.

Baked Beans III

Ingredients

1 (28 ounce) can baked beans

1/2 pound bacon, cut into small pieces

8 ounces brown sugar

Directions

⮎ Preheat oven to 400 degrees F (200 degrees C).

⮎ Pour beans into a 2 quart casserole dish.

⮎ Place bacon in a 9 inch skillet, completely covering bottom of pan. Spread brown sugar over bacon and cook on medium heat.

⮎ When bacon grease starts to bubble up through the sugar, transfer to the casserole dish and mix with beans.

⮎ Bake in preheated oven for 45 minutes.

Marlee's Clam Chowder

Ingredients

8 slices bacon

1 cup chopped onion

1 cup chopped celery

7 cups clam juice

3 (28 ounce) cans stewed tomatoes

5 tablespoons dried thyme

2 (6.5 ounce) cans minced clams

Directions

- In a large pot over medium heat, cook bacon until crisp.
- Remove and crumble.
- Return to pot with onion and celery and cook until onion is translucent.
- Stir in clam juice and tomatoes.
- Season with thyme and pour in clams.
- Simmer 45 minutes, until flavors are well blended.

Shrimp Gabriella

Ingredients

12 large shrimp

6 ounces provolone cheese, cut into 12 strips

1/4 cup green chile peppers, diced

6 slices bacon, cut in half

1/4 cup barbecue sauce

Directions

- Peel, devein and butterfly the shrimp or prawns. (To butterfly shrimp: Split shrimp down the center, cutting almost completely through.)

- Insert a strip of provolone cheese and 1 teaspoon of the diced green chilies into each shrimp. Fold over the shrimp and wrap with a half strip of bacon. Secure with wooden picks.

- Cook shrimp on grill, basting with your favorite barbecue sauce, until bacon is cooked and shrimp is pink.

Shrimp Kisses

Ingredients

1 (8 ounce) package Monterey Jack cheese, cut into strips

40 large shrimp - peeled, deveined and butterflied

20 slices bacon, cut in half

Directions

- Preheat the oven to 450 degrees F (220 degrees C).

- Place a small piece of cheese into the butterflied opening of each shrimp.

- Wrap half of a slice of bacon around each one to conceal the cheese, securing with toothpicks.

- Place on a cookie sheet.

- Bake for 10 to 15 minutes in the preheated oven, until bacon is browned.

BLT Bow Tie Pasta Salad

Ingredients

2 1/2 cups uncooked bow tie pasta

6 cups torn romaine

1 1/2 cups cubed cooked chicken breast

1 medium tomato, diced

4 bacon strips, cooked and crumbled

1/3 cup reduced-fat mayonnaise 1/4 cup water

1 tablespoon barbecue sauce

1 1/2 teaspoons white vinegar 1/4 teaspoon pepper

Directions

- ⮑ Cook pasta according to package directions. Drain and rinse under cold water.

- ⮑ In a large serving bowl, combine the pasta, romaine, chicken, tomato and bacon. In a small bowl, whisk together the mayonnaise, water, barbecue sauce, vinegar and pepper.

- ⮑ Pour over pasta mixture; toss to coat evenly. Serve immediately.

Potato Casserole I

Ingredients

2 (2 pound) packages frozen hash brown potatoes

1/2 cup chopped onion

2 (10.75 ounce) cans condensed cream of chicken soup

1 (10.75 ounce) can condensed cream of mushroom soup

2 tablespoons chopped fresh chives

1/4 pound butter, melted

1 (8 ounce) container sour cream 1/2 cup shredded sharp Cheddar cheese

1 tablespoon bacon bits (optional) 1/2 cup crushed potato chips

Directions

- Preheat oven to 350 degrees F (175 degrees C).
- In a six quart casserole dish, mix together the hashbrowns, onion, chicken soup, mushroom soup, chives, butter, sour cream and cheese.
- Bake covered for 45 minutes.
- Remove from oven, sprinkle with bacon and potato chips. Bake uncovered for 15 to 25 minutes.

BLT Pizza

Ingredients

4 slices bacon

1 (10 ounce) can refrigerated pizza crust dough

1 teaspoon olive oil

2 cups mozzarella cheese, shredded

1 tomato, chopped

2 cups shredded iceberg lettuce

2 tablespoons mayonnaise, or to taste

salt and pepper to taste

Directions

- Preheat the oven to 375 degrees F (190 degrees C), or according to package directions for pizza dough.

- Place bacon in a heavy skillet over medium-high heat, and fry until browned, but not crisp. Drain on paper towels.

- Stretch pizza dough out over a pizza stone, pan, or cookie sheet.

- Brush the dough with olive oil. Spread the shredded mozzarella over the crust, and arrange the tomatoes over the cheese.

- Chop bacon, and sprinkle evenly over the pizza.

- Bake pizza for 10 to 15 minutes in the preheated oven, until the crust is golden and cheese is melted in the center.

- While the pizza is in the oven, toss the shredded lettuce with mayonnaise, and season lightly with salt and pepper.

- Top the finished pizza with the dressed lettuce, and serve immediately.

Sunchoke and Sausage Soup

Ingredients

4 slices turkey bacon, diced

1 (16 ounce) package turkey sausage, casings discarded, coarsely chopped

1 pound Jerusalem artichokes, peeled, halved, and cut into 1/2-inch slices

6 small white potatoes, peeled and halved

3 stalks celery, diced

1/2 large onion, diced

1 leek, white and light green parts only, chopped

3 cups chopped fresh spinach

2 cloves garlic, minced

1 quart chicken stock

1/2 cup chopped fresh parsley

2 tablespoons chopped fresh basil

2 tablespoons chopped fresh oregano

1 pinch cayenne pepper

1 pinch ground paprika

salt and pepper to taste

1/4 cup all-purpose flour

1 cup water

Directions

- Place the turkey bacon, turkey sausage, artichokes, potatoes, celery, onion, leek, spinach, and garlic into a large saucepan.

- Pour in the chicken stock, and season with parsley, basil, oregano, cayenne pepper, paprika, salt, and pepper.

- Cover, and bring to a simmer over medium-high heat.

- Reduce heat to medium-low, and simmer45 minutes.

- Stir the flour into the water until no lumps remain. Stir into the simmering soup, and continue simmering, covered, 30 minutes until thickened, stirring occasionally.

Barbecue Butter Beans

Ingredients

2 (15 ounce) cans butter beans, rinsed and drained

3/4 cup packed brown sugar 1/2 cup ketchup

1/2 cup chopped onion

3 bacon strips, diced

Directions

- In a bowl, combine the beans, brown sugar, ketchup and onion.
- Transfer to a greased 1-1/2-qt. baking dish.
- Sprinkle with bacon.
- Bake, uncovered, at 350 degrees for 1-1/2 hours.

Lightning Source UK Ltd.
Milton Keynes UK
UKHW020641090421
381706UK00001B/63